GW01553191

MAY ALL BEINGS ROCK

Prize-winning poet Lawrence Pettener survived the late-70s rock era to be at Led Zeppelin's last UK gig. It left a poet speechless (there are, however, plenty more books on their way).

Having dodged bullets in Liverpool, Turkey and Pakistan, he continued alone overland to India and Nepal, where he taught English to Tibetan children. He also survived fruitarianism, cave life, Israeli workcamps, deserts, intentional communities, tofu, the new age, London squats, modelling, teaching refugees English, cats, relationships, shared houses, care work, call centres, qigong and fridges full of chocolate (though not necessarily in that order). He is now celebrating middle age and writing in Malaysia. Apart from working on his own creative projects, he helps clients on a range of writing and proofreading work.

He identifies strongly with being Liverpool-Irish, as well as European. Liverpool exerts a strong influence on his poetry, as does place in general. Publications include an audiocassette collection and a weekly page (reviews, interviews) in *The Bath Chronicle*.

His work is best known in European capitals, where he has given many live readings and had his work translated widely (including into Gaeilge/Irish). He has also given BBC broadcasts.

Lawrence Pettener has an M.A. in Creative Writing from Bath Spa University. He has taught Creative Writing at UWE and other UK venues.

His writing website is www.lawrencepettener.com

LAWRENCE PETTENER

MAY ALL BEINGS ROCK

To CTR, SMR and APC

ACKNOWLEDGEMENTS

Thanks are due to the editors of the following publications:

Crosby Herald; Crosby Journal; Decode; Helicon (2 poems); www.intellectbooks.co.uk; Interpreter's House; Liverpool Echo; nthposition (2 poems); Pimp$ of the Alphab£t Press; Sepia; Stationa/ery (US); Strawberry Duck; Tuba Mirum Spargens Sonum; Urthona (3 poems).

Kali's Domain won first prize in Helicon's annual competition for Bristol University's Student Media Awards, best poem 2006. *Young Buck* appears in *New Friends Betjamen Tribute* (Parkinson's Disease Society/Bath Spa University), September 2006.

For bringing me along in my writing, I would like to thank Tim Liardet, Gerard Woodward and Carrie Etter at Bath Spa, plus Philip Gross, John Burnside, Katherine Pierrepoint, Ted Hughes and David Bateman (in reverse chronology).

I am grateful for pertinent conversations and/or email exchanges with Michael Donaghy, Les Murray, Pascale Petit, Don Paterson, Fiona Sampson, Neil Rollinson, Phillip Lyons, David Briggs, Nicholas James, Carole Humphreys, Thomas Osborne and Amy Lomas-Coles.

Thanks are especially due to Yivei Pettener whose loving support and unquantifiable help have made this book possible.

CONTENTS

Dances the Rest of Us Never Learned
In Memoriam, Michael Donaghy

The Lamb and Lion after readings
with the others, all northerners but you
who were from nowhere and now here,
plus New York, Eire, London, all at once.

Grinning, glint-eyed and boyish, your readings
were the sound of trees growing; never
the safest, you memorised all your material,
rhyming or not, as we all dreamt of

and you perfected with feverish care.
The lengthy anecdotes and wide toothy grins;
the round boyish head, deflecting age-guesses;
an alternative to predictable

'alternatives'. Pacing your rhymes' rhythms,
you bridged all the gaps, between page and stage
at the very least; dancing in each,
holding us forever through tongue-in-cheek,

the ponderous, and then that final horizon
you faced suddenly alone, without stopping
to taste autumn vinegar; leaving the rest
of us to catch our breaths and wonder

what part of 'yes' it is we think we understand.

A Couplet or Two on Duality
In Memoriam, Charlie Blacklock, 1967-2007

Poetry never has reason to rhyme
though not many things are true all the time.

Each moment a massive celebration –
we tear up and trample the invitation.

Dig through deepest shit to find fullness flowing –
gold in the graveyard darkly glowing.

Winds howl, life's intense; gaps between the gusts
support the thin fact of existence.

May all beings rock, may all beings roll;
may all beings bop till they drop the goal.

May all beings find spiritual friends
for longer than their singular lives; this is the end.

The Suppression of Poetry
In Memoriam, Ted Hughes, 1930-1989

Poetry is dead. Long live poetry! We can live
without it, you and me, or exist. Leave it out,
forget it; let it rotting, grow its own way
underneath your underground
alternative mediocrity.

Poetry is best suppressed by Radio 1
Atlantic forked tongue and rivermouth
manip you nod when I do, yeah?
And poetry's as well suppressed by the struggle to be free
as by the fascist in you and in me.

And who's protected? Poor poetry? Look, listen,
poems rage like elements; their bite
is worse than a critic's,
they cut rhyme's reason clean out.
They eat cinders, roots, live sense organs.

Poetry is dead – long live poetry! As drama and fiction
move in on its territory, poets lay down pens
and start barking —
far too few poets to pacify me.
Poetry is dead – long live poetry!

The Heart of Sadness and the Start of Hardness

Each moment, a tremendous celebration.
As the earth around us starts to shake
we tear up and trample the invitation.

At moments too numinous to mention,
emptiness and luminosity make
each moment a tremendous celebration.

The ground swells, the room fills with emotion.
Fear levels rise as the ground quakes;
we tear up and trample the invitation.

Another moment, fed up now with caution,
releasing the grip is all it takes;
each moment a tremendous celebration.

Then elegance elides into relegation;
'dignity' digs tiny holes for our own sakes.
We tear up and trample the invitation.

Noses up, we sniff with suspicion
the oysters that are served to us on plates.
Each moment a tremendous celebration;
we tear up and trample the invitation.

Losing a Body

After sitting still in meetings
for an hour or more, you move to stand up,
and everything is utterly gone. All sound

backs off while your blood takes a break;
in behind you, the room whirls softly
in graphic shadow. You manage to nod

at uncertain places, smooth your chin
to look thoughtful, and make your hands invent
a pretext to sit, in case you collapse.

Once, in Katmandu, your mouth flew open
and a spirit entered. You woke with a gash
above your eye, recalling nothing.

Next day, in Hari's café, Mad Rick saw you
before you saw him – again, apparently.
Rick should have been someone's hero;

he would start a smack clinic in Sydney
with money raised by smuggling smack.
He told how you had flown at him, fully inspired –

like a madman, he said, in a spirit body;
how he flattened you with one good punch
to give you back your body, and that kind cut.

Brightloaded

You walk out alone,
listening the park;

lines of trees
run right through you.

Exhalations, you follow all the way.
The whole lot disperses,

as branches and leaves
orchestrate space

in this low autumn light –
everything's edges

stand out now,
as though to meet you –

familiar, this, somehow,
this quality of presence,

like cats curled up
into the dream's inner edge.

Has it always been like *this*, you wonder?

Black Light

This poem makes conscious use of phrases employed
in *The Orchid Thief,* by Susan Orlean, Ballantine 2000

It's hard to tell you what an orchid is,
you just have to be around them. They're
chameleons of the plant world: they can smell
like rotting meat; cake; chocolate, or other flowers.
They can look like birds, lizards, insects and clowns.
Tortoises, toads and monkeys too.

They can feel like human flesh, some of them;
artists, every one of them, to turn out
like that. Yes, we can grow them to order.

You gotta be some weirdo to stick
this business; yeah, I've been at it years now.
No, I do not discuss what I did before.
Look it, we got all kinds of ways to coax
them to grow; Day-Glo paint and other stuff
I wouldn't want to tell you about.

Look,

they become their true selves in black light.

This Tap Behaviour

As I close my door, my psychotic neighbour
bangs the wall just once to let me know he's in.
I move to fill the kettle. He goes at his taps
with a hammer, or fists perhaps.

It disconcerts me mildly, though this
is the light end of his range – he runs
to shouted threats, fists ground in my face
in the street. I call it obsessive compulsive,

this tap behaviour – a colleague said it must be.
One night last week, his tap seemed to stick –
he may have left it open, I thought, unusually.
I imagined him stopped still and listening

to it too – there was no noise coming through,
just this plangent song of water, a plumbed release
of pressure. A long, pining whine keened high
through our shared pipes like sacred music.

Yat Kha

Yat Kha are the best Mongolian punk band
I've ever seen; the only one, in fact. And since
we're talking facts, they're neither punk
nor Mongolian; they're unique. Listen,
they're from Tuva next to Mongolia,
three days' haul from Moscow – far out indeed.
Heavy versions of traditional folk songs
and covers of western rock classics

are thrashed out on goat-hair violins,
drums, and Albert's electric guitar.
Albert's throat singing is what wings this band
out. Lemmy, Barry White, anyone

is falsetto compared to this. Close your eyes,
and a herd of Hondas, Yamahas
or Suzukis are calling out to each other
as they graze the steppe.

With fuzz-box and phase, and seemingly
from nowhere, winds skirl by the carved horses
on the Tuvan instruments. The crowd, aged
from nine to ninety, goes wild. Albert smiles

and makes deadpan comments between numbers,
a Steppenwolf in biker's leathers. We
drink Guinness afterwards, at the bar – not quite
as wild as fermented mare's milk vodka.

Drinking John Burnside's Beer

After sitting around, we heard you say
"Let's go to the pub – the drinks are on me."

You had thrown out the invite
at ten forty-five on a Thursday night

and the pub was half a mile away, uphill;
a driech night, but just a smirr of rainfall

fell, and I got there two minutes late
in time to hear the landlord say

"You're taking the piss," and
to save you from embarrassment

with a fiver for the takeout.
So we stayed for the lock-in and talked about

Neil Rollinson and Matthew Sweeney,
being Celtic and sensuality

before getting back to the fire,
where four brown bottles of bitter

balanced in the heel of the night.
We shared secrets we would not

remember telling; all drank the silence from each other,
reached poetic states. Cheers for Timothy Taylor's,

John; how good it was, you might never know
'cause you were outside with the smoking crew;

wine-glass in one hand, yourself in a swither
your cigar burning fiercely in the other.

From your state of fullness, I think you allowed
me to take back in some of my shadow.

In Praise of Chips

The underground network of eyes
supports and nurtures. Each assists
the others in the leaching out of poisons
earthed by neutral dark space.

When the time is right, the whole lot
is lifted, separated and washed. Comforts
are installed with the stirring-in of milk,
butter and pepper, and fluffing up
the mushy mass — or it emerges
in fast-food outlets in cities such as London
or Liverpool —

where your man, eight pints down, slurs
waspishly to his wife: "*D'yer wan' chips?*"
"*Yer wha'?*", his wife replies. He repeats
the seeming slur. She nods, consentingly.

Salt and vinegar are applied
and it is held aloft above the queue,
to be passed on like an Olympic flame —

Subterfuge

I once got my best friends round for a meal
and for afters there was a special treat,
something fridge-set.

The outside was plainly dark chocolate,
but when they tweaked each stump off the plate
with their thumb-nails

a white knuckle showed through below.
They knew what it was immediately: garlic.
Even though they'd suspected

I would try something like this, they were appalled.
I had parboiled the naked cloves and then hacked them up.
You'd think

I had murdered somebody, and here was the proof.
Their shock surprised me – moreso, their refusal
to partake. Suddenly defensive

now, I thought up the lie I've used ever since:
that I saw the Swiss chef Anton Mosiman
cooking it, on T.V.

News from Europe

The Berlin chocolate shop, years
before they popped up in England
like acne: a dark one with little
red peppers; white, if you can call that chocolate,
with poppy seeds; one with dill
and green pepper; espresso,
full of beans; and one
with rosemary and cinnamon.

The peppery one popped properly
in my dropped jaw. The impure white
crunched happily, and poppily; the dill
grew on me greenly, with all due diligence.
Espresso expressed itself for hours,
and later that night. The herb one
balanced its flavours on my tongue:
Rosmarin und Zimt (rosemary and cinnamon).

But how could I begin to break it
to people back home?
I imagined chunky sushi choc,
and rhino and gooseberry.
For traditional chocaholics
there could be salt and vinegar
perhaps, plus cheese 'n' onion
and white with English mustard.

Seventy Percent

With supermarket *bogof* deals,
you build up a little collection.
The spines, a hundred grammes thin,
stand out on your shelf, slim volumes of poetry

for the young tongue to get itself around.
Some look good and impress friends; others
are for digesting whole. This one, in black
and white packaging and foil glindt,

is the best consistency your callow tongue
has brailled. Much thicker than the others,
one seems encyclopedic; it's a box
of them, a chocolate anthology:

the *Collected*, or perhaps the *Selected*.
They're not always predictable, though
the white ones will be as controversial
as a sudden claim of authorship.

While its purity may be noted and valued,
when you eat it alone the whole lot will slip down,
bittersweet as good poetry. The taste
for bitterness comes later on in life.

We All Need Support

We went to see the big man, God
to my friends, at the Olympic Stadium;
I wasn't so sure about this star; I liked
the acoustic stuff he did before
they say he Judased forth. It helped
that the tickets cost a fraction
of what they would have done in England.

When his Bobness took the stage, my friends went mild.
He hardly looked up over the flock at all,
not like Carlos had, and Joan too, earlier
in the day. I thought it was just me
struggling to identify the songs
from the gravel drawl's aggregate, till I noticed
my friends conferring.

I recalled playing his *Budokan* discs
in our living room, before swapping them
with friends. My mother had asked me: "*Is this
one of your friends, drunk*?" Teenage, I feigned disgust.

This time though, maybe three years later,
I was in no such mood. Joan and Carlos came on
to play with him, saving the gig once again.
Later, leaving the venue through concrete
subways, we found a busker sitting on the ground
as in a festival field, playing clear,
authentic versions of Bob's songs.
Not only that, he knew how to talk.

We adored him. He spoiled it for one
of my friends though, a lifelong Dylan fan,
by looking up and smiling.

Classics in Three Movements

1. Moderato
As I'm texting back my recent ex
to say it's such a shame she can't continue it,
my nineteen-year-old neighbour across the gardens
performs a slow breast inspection right up
to the window. There's not much to examine,

which is how I like it; just enough to feed my imagination.
As I start to engage, there is movement
in another window. Though no-one on that row

will see the middle of my body, the thought
of her eyes and mine meeting at the critical moment,
excites me. The movement in the room, the house

next to hers, begins to distract me, and I check again
that the window-sill covers up above my navel.
I catch a to-and-fro arm movement, held far higher,
as her neighbour practises violin at a slow tempo
similar to mine. I can't begin to imagine what it is
that he's playing. Now she's blurring

2. Oscura
...into the shower. I can't see anything,
but carry on playing my flute to the tune
coming out of my computer: *Whole Lotta Love*.

The bathroom misting up, reminds me
of Motorhead's stage set on the *Bomber* tour
(1978) in dry ice.

3. Alegria/Fast
After all the music we've faced,
it would be indecent if she were to disappear
into the towel she's using now. Thankfully,
the theme is reprised while she's still wet.
With one arm folded into her middle

her hand's going in and out her mouth
furiously, her head's down and her cheek
is nicely rounded to take her toothbrush.
Her small chest-flags flap; I keep up,
just about, without any accompaniment.
As her teeth come clean I spot
white stuff all around her mouth
and the whole show is rocking: *all white now*.

Deep Purple
(Liverpool, June 2 2002)

Swanned in the Swan Inn
trying to look like I was looking for somebody
who might have died a long time since.
Leather creaks as pedestrian bikers,
born to drink mild, blow dust
off the tops of their pints.
It's Madame Tussauds
with bells on,
and I'm the exhibit heading for the bog.
As I come out they're still staring
and the antique jukebox rocks with *Speed King*.
One sod shoots daggers with his eyes –
"*Yeah, I'm a Speed King*" –
see me fly.

Bjorkquake

Bjork lying on her bed, reading happily
in her hotel room in Los Angeles.

Brrrmmmmm... what's that? Wait –
it's a Bjork-shattering *earth*quake!

Bjork trolleying across the room
in a transport of delight. Brrrmmm!

"*Yes! Yes! Yes!*"
she screams, with

her mouth open wide
enough to swallow a mic.

The world could have ended
and it just would not have mattered;

Bjork had found the perfect bass-note,
the earth-deep sound that Odin wrote

...at last! She'd been waiting
all her life just for this meeting

with her fate. Shame not to record it though –
or was that how she got that sound on '*Pluto*'?

Magpie

I was looking out my window as I always do
on my birthday, looking for an indication,
a flavour of the year ahead – a curiously-
shaped cloud, say, or bird behaviour.

Outside, a magpie landed on my motorbike.
Hello, Mr. Magpie, I sang at him.
He looked mischievously at me,
then another landed – two for joy.
Then another – three for a girl. I was
looking for a girlfriend, so I was happy
to leave it there, but then another landed.

When the fifth, sixth and seventh
appeared, I started to sing the *Magpie*
song. I had the impression
they were all looking at me,
but I couldn't say for sure.

I glanced away momentarily.
When I looked back, they were crowding
round the bike – I counted twenty-four.
They seemed to be organising – two
on each handlebar-grip, and most of the rest
on the kick-start mechanism.
Two were hotwiring the ignition.

I legged it downstairs in two leaps. My bike
was revving up nicely as I flung the door open,

and as I reached the pavement the bastards
were banking round the street corner. I blamed
myself for shining up the chrome the previous day –
the day before my birthday.

Cat Nature

We spend timeless segments of spring afternoons
meditating, silently transmitting to the cat
just how beautiful, how amazing the birds are.

The cat just keeps on smiling. We hope and assume
that he "gets it" the way he seems to get everything else –
birds, for instance. We carry on meditating.

Later, finding dandelion-head tails of bunnies
in the hall, I imagine a meditation teacher
tearing aspirants' flesh from the bone during

otherwise silent sittings – to demonstrate
the temporary nature of existence.

From *Nine Cat-Herding Pictures*

1.
You can lead a cat to water, but you can't
make a cat drink (unless you have
a fairly big liquidiser, that is).

3.
I used to think the plural of *cats* was *cattle*
till I tried to herd them.

4.
Trying to milk them
put the final full stop on it.
I thought their miaowing
sounded like some sort of mooing.

5.
I asked my meditation teacher
the difference between cows and cats.
He told me: Cats are more feline,
whereas cows are – well, more bovine.

7.
Hundreds of cats at Rome's Colosseo
in the mid-seventies, a tabby wave
(reincarnations of slain lions)
clambering as one
for our packed lunch scraps.
I listened carefully
for the Italian 'a' at the end
of their 'miaow' sound.

9.
All these pointless runs he makes
as a commentator would say,
for a striker who's not being supplied
by his team. When it comes to dinner-time,
wet-food highlight of the long day,
he leads me to the kitchen
and the fridge.

Bertha

Blind old cat tightrope-
walking chickenwire fence –
no chicken in sight.

Low Doors

When I see a couple of cats
and I guess she's fucking him and she
or both of them are using a cat-flap,
I know this is paradise

every older cat has dreamed of all their lives.
Past and future brushed to both sides
like an outmoded flat cap,
and they're *there*, with nothing to hide,

to lick one another, endlessly. And beyond,
the air is blue with screams and squeals
and is everywhere, and is gone

Spring

Looking past the inert TV,
we watched the ash insinuating
in through the catflap;
small branches caught in–between,
hinting at the world beyond.

The cat mediated
as the limen itself;
bees lived whole lives
in each sitting
of the swarm
of his purring.

The world was awake.

Where I am

Oil spillage on ground
on Stokes Croft
is a splattered peacock
flashing aquamarine –

leaning forward
into the wind,
this is all there is,
this world scrolled
beneath sleek, slick tyres —
coming down
through bike's gears,
fume haze
leaves me watching —

fiery eye raised,
red eyelid
winking into amber,

and I'm gone —

Existential Issues

I was cycling through St. Pauls
where drivers keep to local rules.
I had reached the roundabout
well before the car approaching from my right,
so I went on for the exit straight ahead.

It wasn't the third time, nor the hundredth,
that I'd been cut up right there,
so I wasn't surprised, but I was still shocked.
She wound down her window
and my recitation of the Highway Code

was flattened by her screaming:
"*You're just a bike! You're only a bike!*"
I thought of Flann O'Brien's
The Third Policeman, existential issues.
As she sped off I wondered,
momentarily, what percentage

of me was bicycle, and how much
participation mystique. Perhaps
it would transpire
that I was already dead,
and that things would keep on turning.

& the Groom Wore White

I crashed a party on Cromwell Road
where people danced their feelings
selfconsciously unselfconsciously
or compulsively happily. Alternately.

I rode back to the house
of a couple who had called to complain of the noise
with other party rebels who played flute
with our new host
on her rooftop till 4 a.m.,
Bristol splayed out before us
like a cat wanting stroking.

After chocolate croissants
I couldn't sleep,
and suddenly remembered an invite
to a Zen wedding
where I knew neither bride nor groom
& the saki was warm
& the wine was passed round & round
& the groom wore white
& breakfast flowered with champagne
in the great Chinese restaurant
in King Street; my rusty steed
grazed the cobbles there.

My forgotten hosts,
may your kindnesses to strangers
bring fortune to your marriage!

First Love

You adolesce out into the heart
of the city, where you start
on literature with girls your own
age splayed wide, like the open

hearth back home; where the smiling
bit inside the knee your family
never had a name for, and its smooth,
fascinating line of flexion, moves.

Through all the ins and outs, one thing never fails:
the dark, sweet smell of the thumb below the nail.
Reassuringly, you turn to your empty face
in the old bedside mirror, and say:

First Lesson

She said *C'mere* and grabbed me by the arm
and the shoulder on that same side. She pulled me
against her, the quick blur of her face merging into mine.

Her lips met my own with no tongue intrusion;
they quivered, as though trying to achieve some aim
or objective. *What are you doing?* I asked,

backing off with a step or three. She stopped.
What? she replied, and waited for me to spell it out,
but I didn't know; I was twelve or thirteen.

My mother had managed to pass me something;
a boiled sweet, as it transpired,
but I wasn't sure exactly how it tasted.

Thighs

In response to *Balls,* by Anne McNaughton, in *Pleased to See Me*, Bloodaxe Books 2002

It's the thighs I look for, always:
women in streets, work-places, buses, cafes.
It's the line I imagine, and look for, on the inner
side – the fine line between the knee and the join
with the body, between adduction and abduction,
giving and taking, something and nothing.
How they smile naively when compressed,
squashed into crouches – Brazil nuts and butter.
And cream. Some days, when the light is just right,
it zims off the tops of them to butter her buttocks
goldenly. You could just *roll* in this brilliance
and lustre – to pluck the strings behind that line,
varying the sound that emerges, later,
with different fingering. The skin elides into itself,
kneaded between my fingers like blancmange –
ah, the brisk of it melting against my face.
To see them flobulating when she sits
with her knees up, the flesh hanging down
all wobble and tweak, and juddering like breasts –
intermediaries between ground and heaven,
like nuns or priests.

A Tiny Death

Picking your nose after chopping chillies
is more than a wholefood alternative
to cocaine. Garlic's good

for occasional treats, but if you want
the real thing it's got to be organic chillies.
Some nights,

after reading Baudelaire out loud together,
I buy my girlfriend a vindaloo; afterwards,
I thrash around

while she licks my nostrils clean out,
my limbs passive graveyard petals.
My sneezing

is copious and yogically cleansing.
Still licking, she scratches at my hairline
and my pelvis

rocks me into waves whose edge I ride,
wavering and flailing between focus
and abandon,

before coming
in to a full-on sneeze.

The Traces

Your pouting lips told me the world was good;
the bottom one's curl was the leading edge of something –
some wavelike thing or nothing, where your juices seeped.

You opened up into my trembling hands
as in slow underwater motion. The gods favoured
astonished love, it lasted eight weekends...

As the years went by, I revisited the traces –
the nut-sweet aroma of your sweat, your face;
your breasts, the skim of flesh smooth on flesh.

Your inner thigh, the feel of your name in my mouth.

Statuesque

Mid-afternoon in Karlovy Vary;
we've been here an hour, tired and hungry
off the slow Prague train; long enough to leave
bags down and drink some tea. The sign says
Star Club; we recall the clubs in Prague near
the Zizka monument, were daytime cafes too.

Communication has stalled between Pete
and I; he sits on the car-park gravel.
I go in with my German language memories.

The door clicks shut behind me – *You Sexy Thing*
blares from speakers over the stairs; I'm sure
there was nothing playing till the door clicked shut.

I enter into huge empty club space –
pseudo-suave pastels and not much else
but a woman sitting at a bar facing me.

We nod to each other in an international language.
Do you have any food?
Take a seat, please.

Twelve young beauts appear in leotards
striking poses and pouts. I'm in need
of a different sort of oral experience.

One of their mouths makes a downward curve
as I escape toward the stairs.
Pete remains stone-faced when I tell him.

37

Sarajevo

The cleaner in the launderette
is from Sarajevo;
her eyes look out
from somewhere older than she is,
and her voice has a sad,
Scouse-like lilt, as though

she is singing tears:
I don't know why is it,
she says,
that one sock is left
by the people, always.

I speculate
aloud, that this
is the minimum sacrifice
demanded by the Goddess
of the washing machine.
She nods, appreciatively,
with a faint smile; her eyes
seem to fix on the idea
as I say it. The machine

behind her pounds on
with that timeless, tabla rhythm
like that produced
by *dhobi* washer-workers in India,
and we both sway ever so slightly.

Pantheon

The Basilica of St Maria ad Martyres, Roma

As you step inside, you find it was printed
on the inside of your mind already,
fused with the dome's perfect zero
of the round central skylight.

Somehow, it landed; and continues to do so
into the marble floor's circles and squares.
The walls' concentric squares are windows
on to something, even for non-theists.

In the middle of all this, you lie down on the floor
to allow yourself this give and take.
The dome's resolve is one you could never own:
to keep your life's diameter in line with its height.

Story in Three Words

I went with Julian to Rome.
He became Giuliano, I was Enzo;
we drank coffee for weeks, in training.
I didn't quite hear anyone calling
Mama mia with those stretched, operatic diphthongs,

but I did rename the food we ate
at the restaurant next to the monastery
'*Gnocchi on Heaven's Door*'. The woman
I had chatted with at FNAC bookshop
lived with her parents and said:

"*Ah, you don't know the mens Italians.*"
She flicked her fingers horizontally,
tutting, and changed the subject.
On our last night, we went out for a meal.
In the cubicle behind us, we heard

a guy in his twenties on his mobile phone:
"*Mama... sono mangando*".
That last word's second syllable stretched
into Freudian vistas that girdled
something basic to Italian culture.

At least he could tell her
he was eating somewhere other than home.

Cante Jondo

Tak-takatak, tak-takatak... *Oye!*
Eso es! Yes — this is it: *Siguiriyas*
unfolds from its own centre. We are implicated

deeply, all of us. I am here with Maria, my housemate
from Galicia. It is *demasiado*; we like it too much.
We survive intensely until the interval

like wound-up cats. It begins again
barely visibly, in near-total darkness –
a minute action born from intention, stage right –

a foot pointed outwards, posturing precision,
the inevitable: *dance, sex, tragedy*. The séance
feel of the moment erupts into ribaldry

and lightning for the spine. I shatter
like a brandy glass with shards flying inwards.
No, I am not alright. Later, at home,

I translate Lorca roughly: *You can have*
your psyche torn apart by authentic Flamenco.
Hombre, tell me about it.

The Pouring of Oil

We waited, equal, near Damascus Gate
for the old man to dish out the yoghurt.

The others all had something on theirs
that I didn't. The green something
gulfed with strange viscosity
around their yoghurt mounds,
islanding them; my curiosity cooked there.

Gesturing my arm, I asked for some too.
His moustache covering his surprise,
he poured the green gold on, like balm.

Electric in colour, it glowed on the plate
with memories beyond my skin; it pushed
my rigid teen boundaries. But these Arab men
were not embarrassed, and neither was I.

Smelling slightly musty and just
somewhat unfamiliar, it brimmed
against the well-formed substance
like a warm, protecting sea.

Basic Goodness

Once, in South Tyrol, I waited in the dawn
between lifts; narrow road through a mountain pass,
high Alps around me like a brother's shoulders.

I asked the eventual driver
how long he'd been waiting for me,
then promptly fell asleep.

He woke me where I needed to be.
The world was waiting, intact.

So Much for Common Sense

At Victoria Station I slowed down
when I heard a young guy on his mobile, say:
"There's so much people." I recoiled for a second
and a wavelet ran through my sacrum; something
took permission to unlock, as an Asian family
stepped all around me. When a mother and her train

of kids flowed into my trailing jacket,
my day-pack merged with the German
hiker's rucksack, and all eyes elided,
looking up to find a platform together;
and I knew that that young man on his mobile
had been completely correct.

The Communications Age

Come out from behind that mobile
she said,
and talk to me.

Pheasant Struts

past retreat hall window
in time to my head's
incessant music: Zeppelin's *Kashmir*.

Friday's Writing Group –

ten hands taut round twitching pens
trying to let go.

Reincarnation

Neuroses
as compost –
new roses.

Buddha Blues

Well I woke up this morning...
in a manner of speaking.
I lay there, really,
gazing into space.

May all beings rock.

I had woken to find myself
at ninety degrees
to how I'd lain last night –
did it point to something,
I wondered?

May all beings roll.

Thinking's a mindfield,
trying to work out who you weren't in all your past lives;
the thoughts, the moths that imitate them,
why do they come buzzing? To explore
the suffering of electric lightbulbs, it seems.

May all beings bop till they drop.

After that, searching for my favourite song
was emptiness itself, like a starving ghost.

May all beings rock;
May all beings roll.
May all beings bop till they drop the goal.

The Zen Centre

It was in the perfect spot
for a Zen centre,
between a betting shop
and a fried chicken joint
and opposite Brewers' Droop,
the home-brew place.

It was Leonard Cohen's group;
I'd like to have asked him
why he didn't change his surname
to *Koan*.

One night there was a burglary;
they got away empty-handed.
If you break into a Zen centre,
that's the deal:
you get nothing.

Sutra Neti

First thing in the morning
before brushing my teeth
and yoga practice,

I'm at the bathroom sink.
I slide the orange rubber tube,
slimmer than a worm

through the closed left nostril,
pushing softly to penetrate
the swollen lip at the nasal root.

Once I get it through I reach into my mouth
and pull it, ticklish, to and fro
with slow, milking hands.

I do this every day, at least once;
it's almost compulsive. It keeps the nose
clear and tunes the psychic channels;

it also jangles some naughty nerves.
I massage the membranes till they tingle,
a delicate balance between pleasure and pain;

blood might come. I'll always remember
that first intimate moment when I poked it through
with my yoga-teacher – after nearly crying,

I fell in love with her. I still had to learn
vairagya: non-attachment.

Kali's Domain

She lay writhing on the street, untouchable,
an old mother dying. Her mouth full of flies,
a small crowd gathered round her, pointing
and smiling. The humour was human,
not at her expense. My Hindi

was adequate, just, to discern it: *See
how struggling is always present,
even now as Kali comes to her*. She
would have had perhaps an hour to live.
An hour later, down narrow alleyways,

I searched out a makeshift toilet. I turned
a corner on to a kennel full of pups
wagging their tails all around it, and stopped.
My calf had been torn by their mother; blood
had been drawn. Back in 'my' part of Benares,

Westerners told me that to ward off
death from rabies meant getting injected
within ten days – a week, now
(in Katmandu only three days before,
a monkey had bitten my shoulder).

I entertained death for five days. A Westerner
told me of a local man who had died rabidly:
his brothers had boarded his windows and doors,
leaving meals for him under the door. I recalled
asking an old, white-bearded man, as I ran

into Bangalore station, what the time was.
He stopped and stood still and put his bags down.
I struggled to slow down to listen. Taking the *bidi*
from his mouth, he looked upwards, and said:
"*Time...*"

No Escape

When I'd finished sitting
to set my mind up for the day,
I switched my hand across the shrine flame
then swiped deftly back across
the way I'd watched my teacher do it
to usher it into its next life.

Grey wax swathes dulled across my desk,
on my laptop monitor,
and even on the keyboard.

I scraped most of it off,
save that stuck in awkward crannies.
I managed to laugh at myself
finding the option sealed off forever
when I pushed at the *escape* button.

Focusing

By the time I account for the single
foreign coin on the desk's furthest corner,
marinading in dust, plus those bits
of broken fingernail
and the tangled cluster of hairs,
everything has been devalued.

From my seat by the window I hear birds,
sparrows perhaps. Sharpening my focus, all I see
is six years' dirt clagging up the window
like a mundane revelation.

As though anything needs to be solved;
I love the bite of this room's cold. In rain
the wetness saturates my mind afresh.
When wind shakes the windows, fiercely,
the sound is all till the back yard re-emerges.
Perfect, this emptiness the sparrow's cry amplifies.

I say *yes* to the slow space that burns
in my chest; hold it lightly
and let it sing
its wider picture.

Sitting at the window still,
I listen to a world in self-creation:
urban reggae of service sirens;
drivers rushing to become;
crows cawing like the newly born.

Late Shift at the Schopenhauer Café

My LED clock was broken; 6.66, it said.
I'd be damned forever if I arrived late for work.
A pubic calligraphy on the side of the bath
said: *Clean the bath.*

I watched a black and white cat
use a zebra crossing on my way in.
It struck me that here was the one place
where it would easily get knocked down.

The out-turned legs of lads
walking past the park stated openly:
things are just the way they appear.
At the children's play area, white swans

with their beaks tucked in behind their necks
were plastic carrier bags.
Outside the café, I saw a motorbike
that ran on blood; or that's what was written

on the panniers, in large red letters –
I didn't see what its owner was like.
At the café in my break I typed *Nothing*
into Google, and got a million sites.

Another Way of Seeing

When I worked in the mental health ward,
we told the patients tales of nuns on spacehoppers,
and anything else we could think of to entertain ourselves.

Visiting relatives were not amused.
That spring, we watched a man through the window
spraying weedkiller; he wore white protective clothing.

We looked round at each other, knowing we had all seen
and identified a spaceman. From now on,
without a doubt, there would be no such thing

as U.F.Os. Later in the year, one nurse brought in
an unwanted, luminous plastic skeleton.
We didn't want it in the staff room.

He hung it out the window, where it moaned
in the fierce British wind
for the cathartic benefit of all.

A Raucous Solitude

It happened again: I woke just seconds before
my alarm reached the urgent moment. I'd been picking
my nose and it was bloody.

In sleep, I had seen my little finger
twisted in a pencil-sharpener. I opened
the curtains on a big grey screen –

is life a container for days, or is it vice-versa?
I had known these things earlier on, years back,
and had done nothing with them.

My Buddha's eyes postcard had fallen
from the mirror; I didn't know who I was
any more.

Straining through the teabag light of the kitchen
the day might turn sunny and look like a picnic
but I would be in a panic.

When I dropped my cutlery on the draining board
it was two skeletons colliding on a tin roof;
the neighbour's car alarm a swarm of locusts
enduring non-stop mass electric orgasms.

Hope & Anchor

We go to the Hope & Anchor, my peers and I.
Instead of sloping off on my own to drink
herbal tea in some Persian café, I am stuck
with artists dropping the burden of names
and poets hardening against humour. How

awkward we all are together, how disparate;
not even the rising line of Nadja's skirt
can save the situation. I hate endings,
putting off the moment when one will kill

the others off with glib goodbyes and the fear
of being the last one out – always unvoiced.
We leave together, as though being left behind
would mean some final existential nightmare,
or maybe just a headache. What are others for?

My mind founders beneath the low tidal reach
of relationship – the long-lasting ones are those
in silent boats, the sort which have been pulled back in:
empty, cleaned out, no longer smelling of fish.

Wild Life, April, England

Winter was just three weeks back
when I told a Broadmead beggar –
*"Change? Yes please, love,
I'll change into a butterfly."*
She fluttered her long lashes and said:
"Why not open that bottle of wine?"
Without hesitation I declined,
kept it bottled.

A post-party park. I waken
into wild life; a cat trickles by
like a stream of consciousness.
Birds chirp, oblivious.
Trees are ringed by crocii,
nature's graffiti,
voting for the all-night party:
"Spring is here, okay!"
Bees are fuzzy-headed,
 jasmine-tranced.

Young Buck

The day was old, and was wasting.
I hauled myself out of bed
and slouched into the sun.

I walked up on to moorland,
a dry-stone corner by some trees.
A crash, a thud, and then stillness –

not ten metres between us,
this young deer and I.
I could almost see myself

reflected in those forest eyes.
Young, agile, all-seeing in stillness,
all-beating in speed; bucking brilliant,

his every step, and quicker
than a nettle's sting.
Wait till you hear what I thought of him.

Doing Tai Chi with My Father

My father is horizontal, his cheeks
massive and sagging. The coffin lid stands up
against the wall. It is a small jolt
to see my own name, something we shared,

on the coffin lid. I've contemplated
impermanence for years, and this is it.
My Dad was all facts and work, and harder facts.
Now, his legs appear empty under the slope

of his full chest and belly. I decide
it is time to inhabit my body: I stand like a gunslinger,
John Wayne perhaps, my elbows winging out
to the sides, hands ready for anything or nothing.

I allow them to rise together like
a conductor, then separate my arms: *White crane*
spreads wings. Walking backwards, my arms push forwards
to *Repulse monkey*, then it's *Embrace tiger*,

return to mountain. I swear calmly, I see
his eyelids moving, his belly rising and falling;
falling and rising as though it were empty,
then full; full and empty, alternately.

To him, I have always had *cloud hands*;
I didn't *push the boat with the current*.
I always failed to embody, to *grasp*
the sparrow's tail. On these present movements,

my father is again indifferent. He turned
human in the last weeks of his life: finding
little things to approve of, allowing things to pass.
I brush against the flowers in the room...

Sometimes, after a sleepless night, say, I feel
what they're putting out as a sense
in my body, resonant – but these ones are plastic.
Shifting to the right now, my arms surge slowly forward.

Kreuzberger

Looking out from the darkness of the bus, a lit-up
hoarding beamed: *Art in Heaven*. My brother
Ged railed: *"They think they're clever, using
pointless bits of English out of context."*
We were standing outside a fast-food place,
a drunken old man lying at the door.

The old man puked his tongue out
after the grey sludge he had been chewing.
Ged stared from the man back to me, and said,
"I'll have whatever he was having." After
a gulp-long moment, we both gave in
to the scorched Liverpool laughter we had grown

up to. It was Ged's idea to get a burger;
he was ready for performance eating.
The wrist-thin thighs glimpsed during his late-night rants
were nourished by cheap beer alone; there were hops,
malt, and no doubt enough other nutrients
to feed a soul, an imagination.

We had rummaged through the old squatted art palace
at P'berg, and would head back to Ged's flat near Lehrte.
We stepped past the man, now brushing the rubbish
from his chin, and entered the flaming burger joint.
Eyes waited, looking nowhere and reflecting nothing,
hardly even empty. A soft-faced virgin boy,

the last one in Berlin, flipped burgers.
The good citizens waited; the queue
was unholy long. Ged turned to me and said
nothing. When drunk, he would rant
as though anybody else's but his own life
hung on it, but now he was empty, too.

Six weeks later, Ged gave his daughter
the big Christmas present he had hinted at:
her mother, all to herself. They cleanse Berlin's
streets efficiently, by giving alcos antidepressants
(the small print tells you, carefully, not to mix them).

Some of my friends asked, did any good
come of it – my being there, Ged's release
from hurting, anything at all?
I told them, His death broke my heart
                                   open forever

People Made of *This*

after Stevens' *Men Made out of Words*

What could we be without basic goodness,
or the genuine heart of sadness?

Coccoons and ruins — life consists
of direct perception. The human

moment is a scape in which
we enter this perception, touched by this,

by the joyous clamour of victory
and by knowing loss and victory are one.

The whole race is an artist who expresses
the opening perception of experience.

Nine Cemetery Contemplations

And further, monks, as if a monk sees a body dead one, two, or three days; swollen, blue and festering, thrown in the charnel ground, he then applies this perception to his own body thus: "*Verily, also my own body is of the same nature; such it will become and will not escape it.*" Satipatthana Sutta of Gautama the Buddha

1.

As I walked in to school
I saw a mother cat reclaim its kitten's corpse
from a pack of local dogs. She was ready
for the death fight; the dogs were indifferent.

2.

With its almost-metallic smile, Tigger's face
is like a full moon in a fog. He's the latest
Harrier Jump Jet on a vertical leap, and – yiss!! –
he takes one of Britain's last starlings
in his mouth. But I can't sympathise
with his teasing, pawing floor game.

At eight years, watching this cuddlesome cruelty,
I manage to reason – with my father's help –
that as we stroke the cats, the cats get to stroke
the birds. Like spoiled kids on T.V. dramas,
Tigger can't finish what's in front of him.
He throws the starling's corpse through a low,
wilting arc, a travesty of flight –
Let's see you fly now, he grins.

3.

Late twenties wasn't young to us, but at thirteen
we found our French teacher *tres beau*.
We all stared open-mouthed as she stood, or sat,
to watch the flaps of her thighs wave like nations' flags.

Our teacher taught us they have separate words
for 'flesh' and 'meat' in French. Simmo touched
her *derriere* as she bent to correct his work;
she brought him out into the corridor

for a word or two in old-fashioned English.
Afterwards, we teased him about French letters
and private lessons; he rode the infamy proudly,
for what seemed an age. Two months later,

swimming with our mutual classmate, Robbo
at Crosby Marina, Simmo's live body was sliced
screaming through the sluice gates, like horse meat.

4.

It was two friends' birthdays on the same day;
they were eighteen and nineteen. We were
in a country lane the locals said was haunted;
we skidded on some leaves, and crashed.
Rushed in to hospital with a broken nose
I came up out of me just as my blood was
to look down on the handsome nurse, the doctor
and my mother. A voice – my own – said:
"Do you believe in the hereafter?"
"Of course I do," I replied. *"That's all right then"*,
it said, and I was back among the wounded.

5.
Two days after hearing that her son's body
had been identified after the Thai Tsunami,
my neighbour received a postcard from him
with a perfect blonde beach on the front. It read:
I'm in Heaven. I'm having the time of my life.

6.
The first thing I look at in my brother's flat
after his death, is the computer his life
has disappeared in to. The only document

of any sort on his desktop, is one in Word.
It reads: "*Dying is not an activity. Watching
a wind-up toy wind down, the steady decrease*

in energy is actively soothing."
A few days before he died, Ged sent
a CD of film-loops and trial programs

he had assembled, as a Christmas gift.
It included, in his own words: "*Instant
Biorhythm chart, very basic. (and I hope*

mine for the next ten days is wrong!)."
I looked at Ged's chart; each of the lines
had come to an end: mental; emotional; physical.

7.

I was in Liverpool to visit my father
for the last time, I knew.
The hotel owner had been to the same school
as I had, she was three years younger.
All those I could name,
she said, were dead;
all who hadn't gone to poly or uni,
but had stayed on in Seaforth,
Waterloo, even Great Crosby.
Most had succumbed to the early eighties smack
epidemic; the Tories were to blame.

8.

Each time I arrive at the Buddhist Centre bookshop
it is about to close; I need to focus.
I'm looking for a copy of the *Bardo Thotrol,*
The Tibetan Book of the Dead, for my dying father.
There are several different versions; even the least
offputting one will still be the last thing he will read.
For him, reincarnation can only be something condensed,
evaporated; I find one that gets straight
to the different coloured lights one sees at death.
He could still easily reject it as a waste of time.
The shop's about to close again, I hear,
but I need a little longer. With the clank
of keys behind me like blunted bells
I return the book to its shelf and walk
towards the door. What I shout echoes
round my head; no one hears it: "*I'll be back.*"

9.
When you were birthed you cried,
and your whole world was overjoyed.
When you die, we mourn while you may find the great
                                                    liberation –
or just be glad to be reborn.

#0187 - 201117 - C0 - 210/148/4 - PB - DID2033707